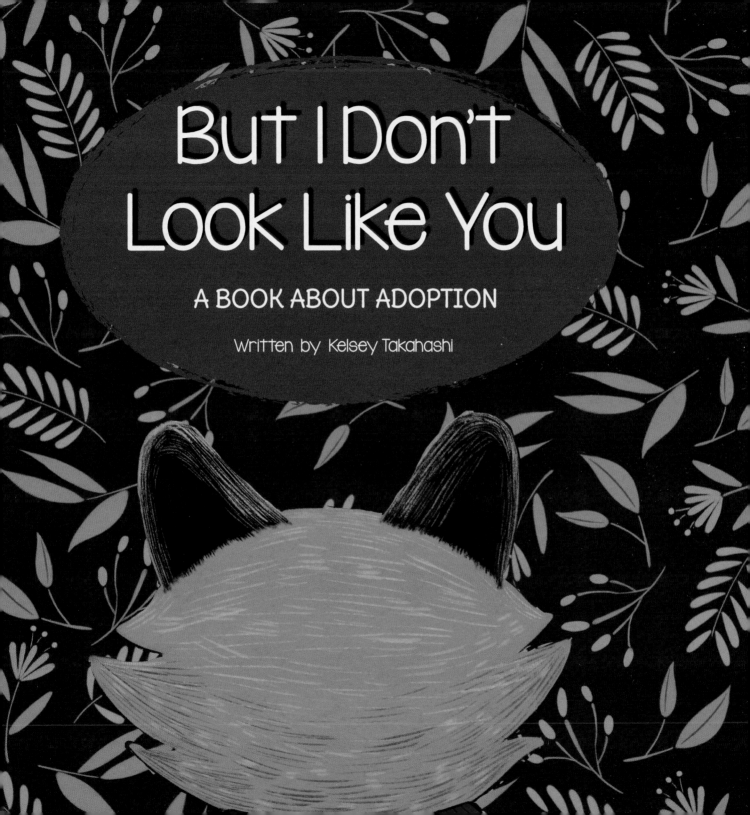

But I Don't Look Like You

A BOOK ABOUT ADOPTION

Written by Kelsey Takahashi

ABOUT

Hello! My name is Kelsey Takahashi and I am very excited to share my book with you. I have an open adoption, meaning I've been in contact with some of my biological family since I can remember. Knowing that each adoptive family has a different story, this book was written to address topics that families with unique backgrounds can explore. The narrative covers conversations that may be difficult to start, like feelings of not belonging, openness about exploring the biological family, and the intentions behind the decision for adoption. Most importantly, however, the love in choosing the option of adoption is a major theme throughout this narrative. This book would have helped me when I was younger because I was the only adopted kid I knew. I wrote each line with the image of my myself dealing with these thoughts, and I hope it will bring comfort to many adoptive families and children too. I hope you will enjoy the story!

With much love,
Kelsey

To:

With love:

I know you are my parents,
but I don't look like you.
Your eyes are green,
but why are mine so blue?

Oh, my baby—
Look in the mirror. What do you see?
There is you and there is me.
It's not how we look that makes us belong,
It's knowing we were meant
to be together all along.

As you grow up,
our differences will stand out.
But just remember LOVE
is what it's all about.
...
You may explore your family
and think, "Where do I come
from and are others like me?"

Wherever it
takes you,
just know from
the start,
your families are
united with love
from the heart.

Some people have babies and
don't feel like they're ready,
so they turn to adoption
to provide a life that's steady.

It was hard for them to let you go. It's a sacrifice of love that is stronger than you know.

There's another family
waiting with hearts open wide
to share all its love and
to always provide.

When that decision is made,
something magical comes true.
Look at my life now!
It has brought me to you.

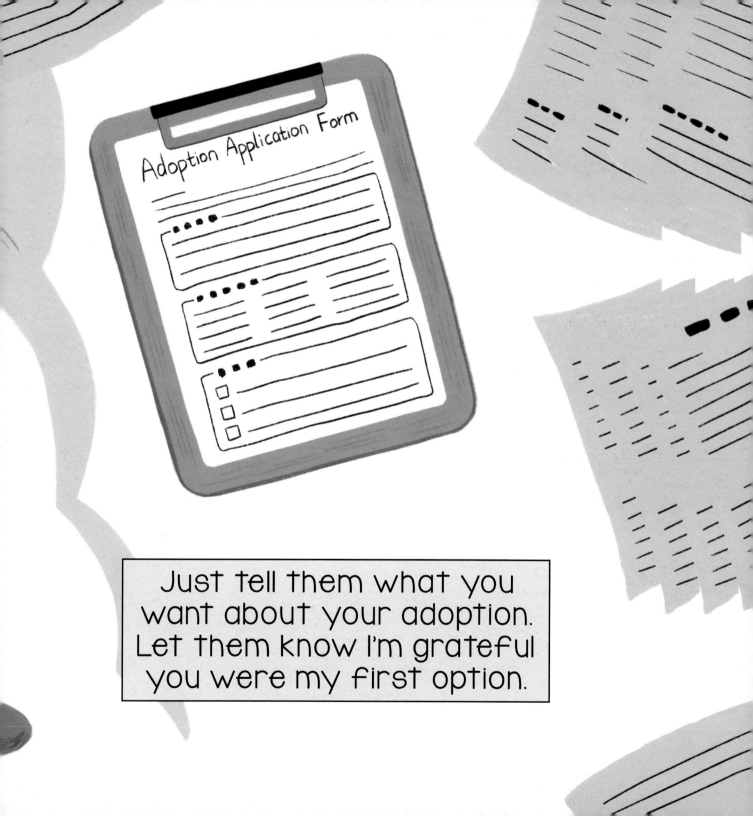

Just tell them what you want about your adoption. Let them know I'm grateful you were my first option.

After hearing all this,
you may want to think.
Silence or talking is alright with me.

If you ever feel
something deep
within your heart,
asking a question is
a good place to start.

So if you look in the mirror
and still think you don't belong,
listen to my words that want
to prove you wrong.

They say,

"_____,

No matter what happens,
know that you are loved.
You will always be my baby,
a gift from above."

MY STORY

What I know about my birth family:

_____

_____

_____

What I know about my birth:

Where I was born: _____

What time I was born: _____

When my adoption became official: _____

Questions I may have about my adoption:

1._____

2._____

3._____

4._____

TERMS

<u>Biological family</u> - People related by blood, also called birth family.

<u>Birth Parent</u>- The person who gave birth to you or you are blood related. This also includes "birth mom," "birth dad," "birth family," or "biological family, mom, or dad."

<u>Adoptive Family</u>- These are your parents and family members. They went through the process of adopting you and you are their baby.

<u>Open Adoption</u>- You have an established relationship with some or all of your biological family since your adoption.

<u>Closed Adoption</u>- At the time of adoption, the biological and adoptive families kept the biological family's information private.

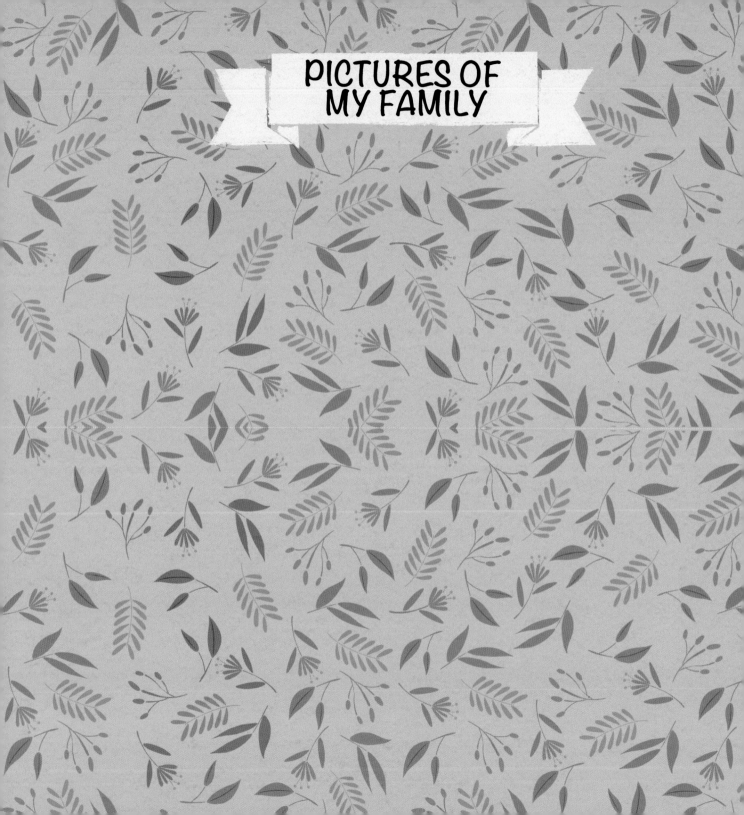

PICTURES OF MY FAMILY

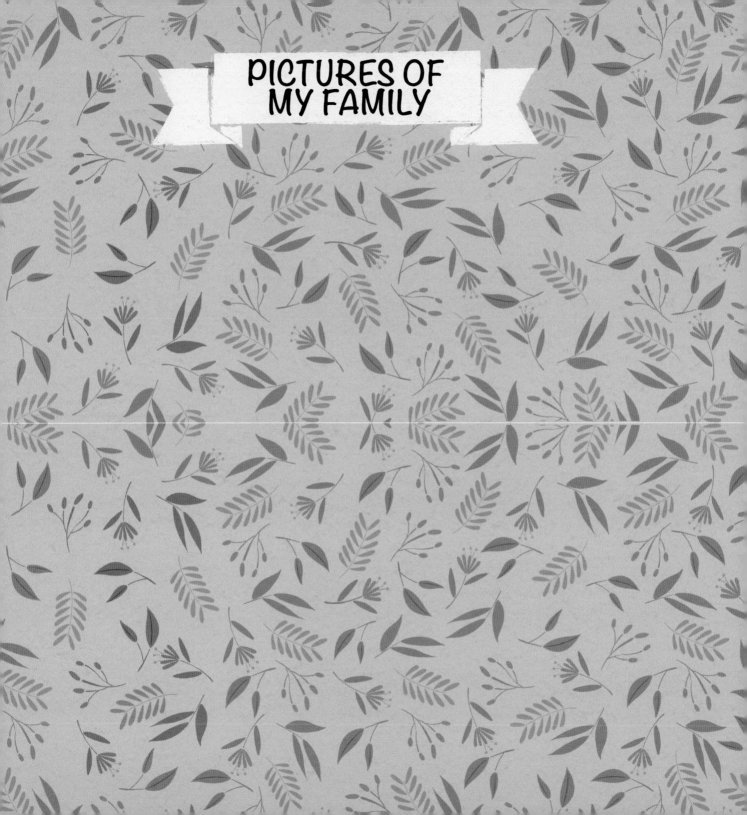

PICTURES OF
MY FAMILY

NOTES & THOUGHTS

NOTES & THOUGHTS

THANK YOU

Thank you to my friends and family for supporting my book. I want to give a special thanks to my mom and dad, Debbie and Roger. I also want to thank my birth-mom, Annie, alongside my birth-dad, Mike, for being part of this process.

ANOTHER
BIG "THANK YOU" TO:

MY FAMILY- Grandpa Don, Aunt Donna & Uncle Tony, Uncle Jim & Aunt Terri, my cousins Travis & Cassie, Hana, David, and Shelley, and my God parents Ed & Jennifer and Steve & Elaine.

MY FRIENDS & SUPPORTERS- Jason, Micayla, Kat, Katie, Andrea, Lynn, Nena, Jacob, Megan, Juan Pablo, Caitlin, Rayna, Tony, Nancy, Carl, Dave & Dannette, Uncle Cliff & Dee, Capri, Connie, Linda, Patty, Chip, Dr. Hanna, Adrienne, Kathleen, Alyssa, Allison, Raleigh, George, Mark, Carol, Chuck & Janis, Mary, Raymond, Julian, Phil, Emily, Eric, Sarah, Erin, Taylor, Saloni, Jennifer, Melissa, Amanda, Robin, Jessika, Emily I, Chelsea, Alyssa, Lisa, John, Arianna, Georgia, Karine, Arby, and Evan.

I am eternally grateful for your support,
Kelsey